Ancients
of the Earth

Ancients of the Earth

Poems of Time

D. A. HICKMAN

Capturing Morning Press

Published by
Capturing Morning Press

Copyright © 2017
by Daisy Ann Hickman

All rights reserved

No part of this book may be reproduced or utilized in any form or by any means, electronic or mechanical, including photocopying, recording, or by any information storage or retrieval system, without specific permission from the publisher.

Print ISBN-13: 978-0-9908423-4-7

Produced in the United States of America

First Edition

capturingmorningpress.com

CMP@capturingmorningpress.com

Logo design © EKM

Cover art © *Sunrise Goose*
Jon Larsen, J & L Photography
fiskr-larsen.pixels.com

Author Photograph
© Jael Studio

Book and cover design
Michele DeFilippo @ 1106 Design.com
Phoenix, Arizona

ACKNOWLEDGEMENTS

My gratitude to the editors of the following publications, in which these poems first appeared. Minor edits may exist.

Always Returning: The Wisdom of Place
   "Always Returning"

Fine Lines Journal
   "Impermanence" – "Sitting" – "This Life"

Pasque Petals, South Dakota State Poetry Society Journal
   "Always Returning" – "Clear-Eyed" – "Listen" – "Pages of History" – "Swift Departure" – "Tall Winds" – "Terribly True" – "Timing"

The Silence of Morning: A Memoir of Time Undone
   "Glide"

Sisters Born, Sisters Found: A Diversity of Voices on Sisterhood
   "Crossing Over" – "Light Show"

South Dakota Magazine
   "If I Must"

VLP Magazine, University of South Dakota
   "Afterlife" – "Higher Order"

BOOKS BY THE AUTHOR

The Silence of Morning: A Memoir of Time Undone

Always Returning: The Wisdom of Place

Where the Heart Resides: Timeless Wisdom of the American Prairie

for ERIN
a joyful free spirit, a beautiful daughter

for JOHN
and 25 years of venerable time travel

Love is what you've been through together.
— James Thurber

*Shape your heart to front the hour,
but dream not that the hours will last.*

—Alfred Lord Tennyson

In memory of Matthew, 1980–2007

"Glide," a poem in this collection, was also included in my memoir of loss and spiritual inquiry: *The Silence of Morning*. Other poems in this collection lovingly retrieve that daunting journey. I imagine that will become apparent to most readers. Now, some ten years in memory, I am deeply heartened to honor my son's life and passing in this way.

In memory of Lola and Noah

A cat, a dog, that came to us at about the same time. To say they grew on us is an understatement. To say they were "like family" is also an understatement. I would wager that creative work is seldom completed without the unconditional love that flows between an artist and beloved pets who never seem to tire of offering their joyful and compassionate companionship. My love and boundless gratitude to both.

Poems of Time

My role in society, or any artist's or poet's role, is to try and express what we all feel. Not to tell people how to feel. Not as a preacher, not as a leader, but as a reflection of us all.

—John Lennon

Ancients of the Earth delves into beginnings, endings, moments lost, then found, that led me to explore the vast influence of time. While a grand illusion, I see myself continually revealed against its fiery glare, even as my awareness of this dynamic has evolved gradually, certainly not in linear fashion. Yet, what is significant (and illuminating) within this dreamlike experience that seems to yield hours, days, years? In 78 poems, fast-paced, like the persistence of a timepiece, I grapple with this question. Like many, I am drawn to time's ubiquitous power, to its inherent mystery: it gives and takes while inevitably leaving us standing alone in the distance. Still wondering, still questioning. While writing a memoir about the rigors of loss, especially the unforgiving weight of time, I also discovered the importance of extricating myself from its steely grip. Not entirely possible, yet there are still ways to intentionally see beyond its barriers. I'm motivated to probe the many tensions and complexities of the human condition for several reasons. My background in sociology is partially responsible, but creative inspiration also flows from my belief in the benefits of a persistent spiritual inquiry into the deepest life mysteries. Awareness can lead to less suffering for all of humanity. Within this framework, these "poems of time" emerged.

—D.A. Hickman

For we are Ancients of the earth,
And in the morning of the times.

—ALFRED LORD TENNYSON, 1809–1892
THE DAY-DREAM ("L'ENVOI" I 19–20)

CONTENTS

*Those who dwell among the beauties and mysteries
of the earth are never alone or weary of life.*
—RACHEL CARSON

I: HUMANITY

Crossing Over   3

Awareness   4

Passages Unforgotten   5

Tall Winds   6

Embracing The Unknown   7

Ghost Avenue   8

This Life   9

Under A Tree   10

Night Voyage   11

Torn Away   12

Fighting Fate   13

Awakening   14

Humanity   15

II: IMPLACABLE

Lost In The Cosmos   *19*
Between Worlds   *20*
Afterlife   *21*
Funny Logic   *22*
Time Undone   *23*
Destiny   *24*
Only This   *25*
Witness   *26*
The Force   *27*
Swift Departure   *28*
Lines Of Reality   *29*
Existential Insight   *30*
Implacable   *31*

III: RESISTANCE

Transient World   *35*
Refusing Surrender   *36*
The Human Condition   *37*
Impermanence   *38*
Curious Resemblance   *39*
Timing   *40*
Cold Precision   *41*
Listen   *42*
Space Time   *43*
Terribly True   *44*
Ripples Of Zen   *45*
Living Mirrors   *46*
Resistance   *47*

IV: SITTING

Higher Order   *51*
Lost In The Clouds   *52*
Subliminal Stirrings   *53*
My Good Fortune   *54*
Antipathy   *55*
Fierce Echo   *56*
Fighting Time   *57*
Courting The Gods   *58*
Among Spirit Walkers   *59*
Stealing Our Steps   *60*
Global Anxiety   *61*
Always Returning   *62*
Sitting   *63*

V: MEDITATION IN BLUE

Secrets Of The Evergreen   *67*
If I Must   *68*
Beyond Folly   *69*
Real Possibilities   *70*
Clear-Eyed   *71*
Creation   *72*
Delicate Connection   *73*
Light Show   *74*
Endings We Feel   *75*
Silent Song   *76*
Strangely True   *77*
Final Wish   *78*
Meditation In Blue   *79*

VI: ANCIENTS OF THE EARTH

Forgiveness *83*

Acumen *84*

Pages Of History *85*

Curious Confluence *87*

Sensing Completion *88*

Missing The Point *89*

The Art Of Remembering *90*

Hearing A Story *91*

Rigged Game *92*

Seeing The World *93*

Glide *94*

A Distant Cry *95*

Ancients Of The Earth *96*

A NOTE FROM THE AUTHOR *97*

ABOUT THE AUTHOR *99*

Ancients *of the* Earth

I
HUMANITY

*The real voyage of discovery consists not in seeking
new landscapes, but in having new eyes.*

—Marcel Proust

Crossing Over

She mailed them to me in a
brown envelope, a clump of
roots with soil clinging to
their sides

I wondered if they carried
hidden life

I wondered how and where
to plant this gift, this daylily.

Red, she'd said the blooms
would be cherry red

an old pail filled with water
became a temporary home
a place for the roots to rest

it seems we all need this
kind of place—

the blooms convinced me.

Awareness

A spinning planet taught me how to
survive the clatter of slow days when
nothing felt authentic; it taught me
to discern a subtle joy, to plant the
delicate stem of peace when closed
eyes could not see, would not open.

A spinning planet held me up as I
came to know the rigors of loss,
how death belongs to me, to you,
like wrinkles and bad breath.

At last this mysterious home pointed
me to a ubiquitous teacher without
fanfare, tension, undue celebration.
A rhythm of dying leaves, the other
day a poignant green, exemplified
an uncomplicated honesty.

Nature's lessons, never muddled
by personalities, politics, division,
never impertinent, despairing, or
empty of promise, ring like a bell
in a steeple of air.

Passages Unforgotten

Same of sky
came the whisper
of evening,
day and night linked

in flight, a heron
sailing across
a lake once
trusted, the one

dissolving into
streams of cold air
that summer night
near daybreak.

Tall Winds

Surely time moves with
the prairie wind,
raking air, together

singing the mystery
of earth,
as though unified in

thought, in purpose,
and hand-in-hand,
a pair of doves,

brilliant, composed.

Embracing The Unknown

If one day was all I had, one tree,
all there ever was, a single morning,
the one and only, would I know it
hadn't been more, maybe a lifetime,
and would I find it incredible just the
same—a life, a day, a perspective of
one, mortality no longer biting at
my ankles, but a notion abandoned?

My question ricocheted like waves
of sudden panic, as I stood shackled
to the ground, the answer hiding
in places unknown.

Ghost Avenue

I felt a stiff breeze that morning
when the elements of an ending

lined up like wooden pins on an
empty clothesline dancing with

an energy I could not name as
the thin white line stood bare

without sheets towels or socks
but idly swaying to random noises

escaping sunken windows in rows
of red brick, the worn farm house

a mere outline of days remembered
like the utter blankness of the hour.

This Life

What did it matter my
knit hat was missing

the forest green one
with yellow stripes

or that only one glove
could be found? The day

was cold but generous, the
air a jumble of snowflakes

finding earth in waves of
chaotic abandon. Stepping

outside to absorb the sun's
hidden light, I felt the brilliance

of winter's mind—its soothing
silence, its pervasive presence.

My mortal moorings had roots
elsewhere.

Under A Tree

Dozing beneath the canopy of a Japanese maple,
the ground cool, welcoming, patiently drinking in
dabs of light filtered through thick sunshade, I dared
to visit the intricacies of my life, twists and turns like
a mountain highway, but revelations sought felt distant,
puzzling, as elusive as night dreams. Listening deeply,
I finally yielded to the present moment only to sense
the listless descent of spent time, withering memories
that were no more.

Night Voyage

The half-moon sailed with precision,
swiftness, never bobbing about in gusty
winds on blue-gray waves illuminated by
the thinning sunlight of evening.

Staring at its silent travel, I dared to wonder
about its precise destination, the moon's, that is,
its snow white hull, a sailboat without a mast,
refusing to carve a path I could plainly see.

Torn Away

Depleted colors, streaks of yellow red,
on all those fallen leaves looked like
stacks of paper saved for long letters
never written.

Pulling my wicker chair closer I sat
with that towering oak to catch the
force of autumn while it worked, not
from afar as though separate or

somehow less than transforming—an
ending that shields many beginnings,
an ending met with a dark silent sigh,
wild and furious.

Fighting Fate

An uncertain future
offered itself when he
sat to contemplate
the span of lived years
in this place called home.
A rush of energy
the process of settling in
his mission clear
he claimed the space
took up familiar routines
rarely noticed pockets of time
sneaking in under doors
around windows
scurrying through his walls
and attic like hungry mice.
Entire years vanished:
elaborate constellations
disappearing at daybreak.
Where, he mused, was that
doe-eyed child who tugged so
firmly on long sleeves until he
finally looked down into her eyes?

Awakening

An earthen blanket hides roots, decay,
and bugs tucked away for protection
until the spring rumble begins when
I too throw off woolen blankets, yawn
and stretch. The darkest of days aren't
all there is, after all.

Humanity

Forest trees stand deep in
the midst of a throbbing
emerald sea.

Unaware of their stature,
lissome roots, digging arms
connecting everything seen,
unseen, they blindly wait for
time to run out.

II
IMPLACABLE

The earth is what we all have in common.
—Wendell Barry

Lost In The Cosmos

Like a faraway friend with a secret
not yet revealed, a silent star eyed
me from an inky sky, or so it seemed
trying to come out of a deep sleep
surrounded by towering grasses that
whistled and swayed, my mind fuzzy,
irrational, unable to keep up at all.

Between Worlds

Webs of past lives, a glimpse,
a look, alter perception

maybe a voice speaks with
halting immediacy

yet the insight vanishes,
the dash of power lost

but the wish for more,
an apparent curse of time

returns when a brisk wind
falls against a still morning

and something causes me
to pause more deeply, longingly;

still the feeling dissipates,
the pulse of life rapid,

demanding—an engine
hidden in the recesses

of swirling hours.

Afterlife

Colors in flight roam
the bountiful prairie
like owners of a vast
land, jewels released
by an invisible hand,
a gentle power:
reminding us to take
flight, birds our
musical inspiration—
a resilient creature,
a turned on, jazzed out,
nimble, airborne spectacle—
a peek at our future.

Funny Logic

Sensing an invisible force aligned
with marigolds, mums, apple trees

she trusted it like her oldest friend,
but he moved against it, unyielding,

always pushing his spirit to question
the purpose of it all, even the need

for bare branches when he desired
forests of profuse green, a trail of

pink from fertile lilies, the mellow
comfort of an evening breeze. Too

much to grasp, he'd say. Too vague,
mystical, especially in January when

he felt tired, distant, abducted by the
tentacles of winter.

Time Undone

The sound was unmistakable,
a distant bell chiming,
its tone deep,
somber,
like cold syrup.
Somehow it rustled summer leaves
on oaks lining our street,
trees stretching from concrete
covered roots, their captivity certain
their insistence apparent.
I stood transfixed,
listening, looking,
as the ringing grew faint,
then loudly absent,
like a voice I'd known.

Destiny

Floundering around we miss skyward stalks of
flagrant yellow, grabbing sunlight, inhaling rain,
emitting a subtle aura of hope. A reliable conversion,
our eyes dance over this eloquent process, calling it
impersonal, predictable. What was never seen, a loss
that fans out across the prairie like a gathering storm.

Only This

When does something end
yet begin, invisibly quietly
without fanfare or trumpets

witnessed by no one only
sensed by the silence within,
a transparent hunch forever

alive in one form or another
and secretly pulling us all to
shore once more?

Witness

When it rains the world spins
like polished silver on display,
contentment rising from a
dusty floor—plants, trees, crops,
enriched and proud like giants,
turning death into life,
just like that ... just like that

then darkness drops its curtain,
a night cap of black and white
drawing curious eyes skyward,
and I glean hints of what exists
beyond a makeshift stage of
shifting color, needing rain
to survive, to fuel us onward

us, surface stars by day, kept
warm at night by a fierce energy
that cries out with snowy owls,
great grays, seen and unseen.

The Force

The night
the hour
my world vision
spin lightly
coming, going,
like many tomorrows,
never stopping long
always becoming
something else
maybe unrecognizable
or dark, troubling,
even luminous as each
instant holds me close
then closer.

Swift Departure

Racing about like
flashy cars on a track

knowing time had
pounced, demanding

the cold of winter,
deep abiding snows,

the pale sun of February,
bluebirds, goldfinch, all

birds with migration
in their genetic codes,

sang hasty good-byes
to feeders, baths and hidden

branches they had huddled on
like seasoned football players.

Lines Of Reality

I force a smile when
glancing through days

buried in dust, and I am
certain my newborn son

my child, was here
... mere weeks ago.

A buoyant beginning in
warm hands, yet

held tight by a certain
otherness, my joy,

my love, only a lifeline.

Existential Insight

Overbearing, sky black, long beaks ajar as if sirens blaring, announce the presence of a barn owl trying to steal a nest, but at last the crows swirl up, away … a trail of silence in their wake, bones and feathers jetting off to another crisis. But the secluded owl with its mighty wing span waits for their naïve absence, and the worrisome story of life ensues.

Implacable

Thin layer of light, a message,
fading sunsets, each a story,
yet the dawn still strikes my
mortal eyes with a piercing
rawness: a steely glance.

What should I make of this, and
how will I measure a life, my life,
with this newness forever around me,
firmly pointing to lost lessons
of history and time?

Today is today, that is all I know,
and gazing from winter's window,
all I can do is wait for a morning
that is yesterday and tomorrow,
or something other than this.

III
RESISTANCE

*We are, perhaps, uniquely among the earth's creatures,
the worrying animal. We worry away our lives,
fearing the future, discontent with the present,
unable to take in the idea of dying, unable to sit still.*

—Lewis Thomas

Transient World

Roving about my yard
crouching, silent

your ghost eyes, like stars,
catch my slightest effort

to remain untouched
by another realm

to deny a mysterious
continuum.

But it seemed those bright
eyes were yours

the last time I looked.

Refusing Surrender

Snowflakes meet
the ground

like salt from
a shaker, never

aware of landing
or of a

precise location,
merely gliding

to a stop when
sky runs out,

when the moment
frees them of flight,

and still we believe
our lives are different.

The Human Condition

I imagined something simple,
a thin gold outline against
delicate pink tossed in last
minute like carrots in a salad

and tucked within the edges,
a new life, one knowing nothing
of time until hunger, fear, the
desire for sleep stirred within—

us born a rattle of erupting needs,
like inner alarms, the kind heard
on raging city streets with dangers
apparent, angst and rancor visible

everything but a sweet gentle day.

Impermanence

Searching for myself within the
confines of letters called a name
was futile, a string of letters void
of explanation, empty of feeling,
except for what was remembered
from mornings, even entire days,
hazy with repetition, but when the
afternoon light pierced the glass of
my studio window I reached for my
paints and brushes and there, on
a canvas, I captured my ephemeral
nature in reds browns soft yellows
and a dab of blue.

Curious Resemblance

Suffering overlooked we
pretend all is well

but our attention guides
us, our eyes show us—

it is there, it is real, it is
sealed behind faces

and smiles that look
exactly like ours.

Timing

Dare to dance was what I heard
that forgiving day in June as

shiny leaves whistled against a
gush of wind like meadowlarks

in flight or perched on a country
fence post yet never able to leave

the cottonwood until the autumn
breeze arrived to set them free …

all crisp and curled, shaped anew.

Cold Precision

Winter air, sharp, silver lines
pouncing against naked hours,
its certainty slicing tomorrow into
the thinnest of pieces, daring us
to cling to thin icy branches with
gloveless hands while knowing
everything shifts with a cunning light,
arrivals and departures swirling
about in heavy nightfall.

Listen

Summer on a windswept prairie
catches me off guard, twisting my
sense of surprise into something

I barely trust, yet I know this land
and its secrets: how wildflowers
erupt with only a hint of warmth

how spindly cedar trees scattered
on a rocky incline spell survival

how the deep green of spirit erupts
all around, how sky and grasslands
collide on the horizon to convey a

single truth—this place of prairie
speaks to me without a word.

Space Time

Snaking in under thick blinds
in a dusty back room
the barest stream of sunlight,
a sword from outer space,
pierces time-based reality
without notice or effort and
I feel forced to look within
and well beyond, as though
the two were one.

Terribly True

Feisty pinks, edgy reds: tiny trumpets
that stir my soul with lush visions of new

and hopeful. Yet despite my ardent
desire to hold tight to this spirited,

fragrant landscape, I am sadly certain
it will not last. Prairie earth, doggedly

pulling free of winter's hold, stirs with
a deep certainty beneath my feet, and

like nature's metronome, is fiercely intent
on the ebb and flow of all things seen, unseen

and still to come. So when the time is right,
I must bravely release these vibrant spring

days, the ones I yearn to cling to, for they
are destined to move on without me.

Ripples Of Zen

Blushing swirls of morning sky
release me from yesterday

yet the creep of dawn is lost
on those adrift in dreams

of more to buy, more to do, just
as I invoke a beckoning rock in a

garden of gray pebbles and stone.
There I can sit with life in a willing

nod to eternity—to study the waves,
the circles, of a secret code.

Living Mirrors

Free-flowing willows bow with ease, with grace,
because time stands still in the heart of nature,
but this fine melody goes unnoticed, us, lurching
about like rusty cars on the blink, us, stumbling,
struggling, unwilling to yield or reluctant to accept,
as slender sweeping branches reach for us,
hoping to embrace tired furrowed brows.

Resistance

Spinning in space, legs sadly useless,
ragged emotions churning like an overheated motor,
I am certain I will be consumed by fear,
an insistent mind still tethered to a linear perspective,
unwilling to let go to explore the universal sea;
but I love the land with its trusted beauty—
how it reaches for my hand in spring,
lets me run with the wind as though a bird in flight,
even those sullen boundaries of time that keep
me in place—so I am loath to imagine what else
I might love because it is unknown to me.

IV
SITTING

*It is to be remarked that a good many people are born curiously
unfitted for the fate waiting them on this earth.*

—Joseph Conrad

Higher Order

Lurking behind a lilac bush,
the first of a late spring,
I spotted a trembling twig,
as if coming to life beyond
its capacity—beyond the
entirety of the season—and
racing for a camera, I caught
myself, noticed my impetuous
behavior, and remembered
at last: Nature is timeless

Lost In The Clouds

So high, so imposing, the sky above my
head. Staring at me until a dark-haired
girl of four or five bursts once more
with questions no one seems to answer,
I wonder if I will ever grow into myself,
forbidding a tall wide umbrella to taunt me,
tease me, turn me inside out, or will I laugh
it all away one day, believing it too strange,
this wild expanse overhead, this eggshell
of fluff and tangled blues? If only I knew.

Subliminal Stirrings

Where have I ever gone
but inside the ceaseless
roar of flimsy hours that
leaves us bumping into one
another like showy balloons
on paper strings?

Yet nothing shares the real
story of existence, not even
the grand book of time,
nor uneven minutes that
hang around, filling the air
with a cloying weight or a
petulant silence whispering
long, winding tales in my ears.

My Good Fortune

She'd witnessed the
radiance of sunrise
thousands of times
before I arrived,
my small hands
barely able to receive
her offerings,
but I listened intently
to her eyes,
their blue waves seeping
into my soul,
and there,
young and naïve,
knew myself for the first time.

Antipathy

Powerful words of support went unheard
so determined his flickering light to fade

before my calendar or clock predicted, but
someone in the distance yelled "so what"

while another wrote "too sad" and "so sorry"
or "time will heal" and "find peace in memories"

like I should want trite expressions thrown my way,
like I should bow to time's ugliness

all of it,
a senseless charade cluttering the skyline.

Fierce Echo

As aliens we arrive, robed in
legs and arms, eyes aglow as if
searching for a safe connection
once known, yet forgotten,
but others dance among us
like cornstalks in August
speaking of good and bad,
life and loss, instructing us
to soar like birds set free
in rainbow colors, to grow
tall talented strong and wise
so when death stops by for us
one brisk autumn morning,
we will have known this place
once more.

Fighting Time

Pale pebbles dotted the mountain stream
the clearest water sliding by to places unknown

but he yearned to block the stream, to plant
both feet right there

then he wouldn't be left behind to worry if he
too should be getting along before caught unaware

alone and wandering amidst naked winter
trees—a ghost too frail to fly.

Courting The Gods

Electric winds blew in from
faraway corners
without regard for the
unprotected on open ground
that summer morning of
ephemeral light
when nothing happened
to alter a destiny that
found him alone
in a meadow of green,
anxious and wishing for
a distant shore
where time is benign
neither whimsical nor erratic
but deeply true.

Among Spirit Walkers

Legs of giants with tangled feet drill far into earth
while seeking open sky

an abundant choir of green reveling in light-filled
hours, hinting at knowledge beyond our flimsy grasp

and we love to stroll among these lusty giants,
gazing up, straining to hear secrets whispered in

the dark, leaves passionately whistling a melody
we too want to hum, but our covetous nature

pierces fertile air as the tallest, wisest, loveliest
trees grow silent.

Stealing Our Steps

My footsteps, and yours, traverse
stretches of land like diminutive rowboats
bobbing about the ocean;
each lifetime—an unmarked path,
winding, fleeting, unpreserved,
somehow reminding me of silver dollar pancakes
from patchy morning dreams, intoxicating
but not quite remembered, not really mine,
yet all that can remain.

Global Anxiety

I studied the river
its banks
its wavy flow
its blueness

I could never match
its steady pace

me, too easily flying
off and away

a restless sparrow
failing to notice the stir
of life under its wings.

Always Returning

where did life begin if not
on a return trip ... from
somewhere or something?
like faded white lilies or
autumn leaves that feed
the earth only to return with
the persistence of spring,
life is a basket of motion:
coming back, coming round.

Sitting

Yesterday the brick path to my garden
stood flat and firm against a lush green

I noticed it more deeply as I walked to my
wooden bench engraved with five words

"the obstacle is the path"—a Zen proverb—
and sitting for time unknown, I began to

understand those words in a brighter light,
as though the sky had moved closer.

V
MEDITATION IN BLUE

*You must hear the bird's song without attempting
to render it into nouns and verbs.*

—Ralph Waldo Emerson

Secrets Of The Evergreen

I study you frequently,
how you give without fanfare,
asking not for glory
or public notice,
only that a generous sky
gap wide for your limbs
as you push upward,
jubilant, strong, pointing
to equanimity amidst
the clouds—a distant
world, perhaps, or an
approaching rainstorm.

If I Must

The rooster died last night,
his feathers a flattened robe
a cushion to take him away
somewhere I will not follow

not while wildflowers emerge
amidst open fields, or in
autumn when I am fixated
on winter, its snow and ice

But summer beckons: a sea
of opulent green; a time of
ripened fruit; a celebration
of everything once begun.

Beyond Folly

Notes, lilting, then subdued,
drift from a tilted window,
a cascade of sound billowing
into sleepy morning air like
thick rings of smoke.

Slowing, I stop beneath the
window's ledge to catch each
melodic wave.

Feeling destined to hear the
music of an unknown pianist,
I stand firm against schedules,
deadlines, agendas.

Instead of marching on, I listen
with every fiber of my being;
those rusty bells of time
no longer my master.

Real Possibilities

Where can I find today:
beneath the iron bench
I sat on around noon,
or above the tree line,
birds swooping in and out
to find the surest branch,
the longest view?

Tomorrow, sun at my back,
I will walk to the same shore,
sit on the same bench and
pretend the day has moved,
when it hasn't.

Thinking like this makes me
dizzy.

I'm on a merry-go-round that
begins once, stops once, while
everything else spins in place.

Clear-Eyed

It was true, my Dakota eyes
saw her good side—fierce,
moody skies drawing my
gaze upward, narrow dusty
roads never held fast by
a single map

old cemeteries with bent
trees and deer peering at
me, frozen and silent, so
as not to disturb the dead

miles of Missouri shoreline,
its waters pushing on while
whitecaps pause to dance
with electric prairie winds: a
fanciful, timeless marriage
I can't begin to overlook.

CREATION

An ageless lullaby rang out from the
shores of yesterday, a fierce spring wind
broadcasting a shared mystery in a cloister
of branches and radiant leaves. Drawing me
in, the rush of euphoria, that stirring melody,
I heard it, saw open-eyed beaks, certain,
yet trembling.

Delicate Connection

A second planting, a third,
then a cool, rainy evening

before the hot sun of morning,
a tumbling path charted long ago

as specks of delicate green in
gently raked soil found their

place amidst uneven rows of
thyme basil rosemary parsley.

so I sat, folded legs on smooth
stone, to see if I could glimpse

sage sprouting leaves like wings,
something we both understood.

Light Show

Did you see the moon around midnight,
absorb its persuasive glow, its brilliance,
its assigned place in the sky, and did you

recognize that snowy sphere from years
ago, the same one that left us wide-eyed
as children, dancing in the dark by its light

on a damp summer lawn, and did you feel
a sudden tug, almost like the Earth shifting,
when a thick night sky captured that moon,

hiding it from us, with us so certain it was
gone forever? It was new then, the sights
before our eyes, the myth of days and nights.

Endings We Feel

Not looking for anything at all, planted there in
oversized weeds was the rusty pump handle for
the well no one had used in years, not in years;
yet it was there just the same, waiting for eyes to
expose it or someone to pump water once more.

But that old farmhouse stood empty now, merely
a crumbling container for intrepid memories daring
to ring out beyond its walls as if wishing someone
could resuscitate a time, a place, when people, old
and young, came and went busy with life and oblivious
to tomorrow, assuming things would never change
until a distant date on the sweltering pages of time,
but today, only muted, free-floating sounds like the
scream of a hawk from a nearby field, the sway of
grass no longer mowed, spoke of life.

Even the lone purple iris, scarcely blooming and
hiding near the stooped pear tree, had fallen
prey to time's lonely swagger.

Silent Song

Alone in bed, book cracked,
a quiet alert energy drew me
toward its pale light—distant
yet luminous.

Lifting my eyes, I gazed at the
window …

breathed, waited, held still.

Seemingly alive behind worn
curtains, subdued, but fiercely
intense, such funny opposites
reeled me in through currents
of time, past shaky beginnings,
wretched endings, into a timeless
space I knew as mine …

the whirring silence of eons,
the tireless self beyond eyes
mind sleep and air.

Strangely True

Patiently waiting for me most any time of day,
lively robins in the garden

zipping through our yard,
specks of yellow called goldfinch

choosing the pinnacle of our maple,
the blue jay

calling to me in a long lonesome whistle,
cardinals on flimsy feeders of gray egg cartons

hitting the glass and dropping to the ground,
birds I cannot name

soaring on wind currents to catch a quick ride,
squawking sea gulls

tucking in pencil-thin legs for a long flight home,
great blue herons.

Seeking the sky, there is no ceiling, no time, only
a playground for wings.

All of this, and more, came to me late one evening
from my easy chair where I sat trying to

imagine myself a bird.

Final Wish

My tattered straw hat flew from my head
during a wild summer storm. Leaning into
whistling gusts of wind, I covered my ears
squeezed my eyes clenched my teeth: a child
hoping to hear the soothing melody of shared
laughter. Maybe see the sweet buoyancy of
compassion: that knowing glance conveying
something unspeakable like a river of tears.

Meditation In Blue

Called to the meadow, eerie
night sounds guided him

a siren blaring between city walls
an infant's wail against a tower of
stubborn silence a man without a
home run over in a busy street

then, a fatal sound against
a darkened silence

layers of life polished by sunlight
struck down by something cold—
metallic, unyielding

touching the whole of life, the nexus,
he knew his own loss.

VI
ANCIENTS OF THE EARTH

*Forget not that the earth delights to feel your bare feet
and the winds long to play with your hair.*

—Kahlil Gibran

Forgiveness

Closing his bake shop long ago he still
took inventory every spring. Each item
glittered in its plainness, the somber
notes of a life's work no longer needed.
Blue flowered paper lining pine boards,
a cradle for dusty flour sacks, ceramic
bowls for warm water, yeast and sugar,
coffee beans and tea, unopened jars of
molasses, honey, syrup, sacks of pecans,
almonds, walnuts, tins of cinnamon,
jars of ginger and cloves, dried fruit in
five ounce bags, cotton towels, hot pads,
cookie sheets in seven sizes, shiny cake
pans, a rolling pin with faded red handles,
pie pans of tin, ceramic, and blue glass,
batter bowls, spatulas, biscuit cutters,
frayed cookbooks, pages marked with
paper clips, strips of paper, note cards,
plastic measuring cups and silver spoons,
white candles in a box, tea lights tucked
behind parchment paper, foil, wax paper,
cupcake holders, paper and plastic bags,
bakeware in a plethora of shapes, sizes,
and rainbow colors, hand mixers, three of
them, a nest of stainless steel bowls, and
off to one side, faded seed packets dating
back a dozen years. Selecting marigolds,
that pungent aroma warm in his memory,
he gave the dusty packet a gentle shake
to savor the plaintive whoosh of endings.

Acumen

Like a rushing river, fierce words
tumbled past my ears

Caught by the current, rapid,
sadly tormented

they vanished like hurried
days turned to night

Created in the world of time,
nothing ever withstands

the ancient sanctity of silence.

Pages Of History

Where might that narrow trail disappear to after dark,
the one behind the rickety gray barn, all broken and
sloping to the east? Lying dormant for countless years,
I'd seen it without really seeing it, but now, having truly
noticed, that trail haunted me, teased me, turned up
in my dreams like a persistent toddler.

Layers of dirty snow melted, grass, trees, wildflowers showed
a pale green, and still I avoided that trail, the one beckoning
like a sparkly night star. Surely, I mused, I will start down that
faint pathway, but only in daylight when sun and hopeful sky
shield me from dark, unknown forces.

But my furtive dreams took a surprising turn, generating loud,
rhythmic steps, the kind with an eerie echo, too certain and
determined. I took to that blessed trail the very next day. I'd
had enough of this silly game: no rules or instructions offered,
no other players identified.

Connecting to that dusty, rock-hard floor in old walking shoes,
my thoughts ran ahead of me until the glint of sunshine falling
on random rocks dazzled me and I forgot to think at all. Like
breathing truth itself, I walked faster, worried less, became
one with that trail. Even my destination seemed irrelevant.

Dropping all defenses led me to what I'd resisted: an intrepid
darkness. Squirming against it didn't help; thinking helped even
less. Exhaustion swelled up in me, a birthday balloon losing air
until nothing was left, not even familiar landmarks to gaze upon.
Meadowlarks had gone silent many miles and days ago.

I must have skipped entire seasons, because when I finally thought to glance behind me that pesky trail had grown wild and unkempt, camouflaged by dense weeds, disordered specks of color. Finding my way back was impossible now, of that I felt certain. As certain as lonely, scattered guideposts on the prairie ever permit.

Curious Confluence

Even on a hot windless day, water flecked with
debris moved swiftly, effortlessly, like a motor
without parts, pulled south to its port. Same day,
I ran into an old acquaintance who later vanished
from her hometown; same day, a lasting drought
originated in a part of the world unknown to me.
Though vaguely imagined, I sensed each eternal
moment, the river's relentless flow, the friend's
unexplained absence, the shortage of rain, as one.

Sensing Completion

She planted the vine in too
much shade never thinking it

would take off as if planted properly
in full sun crawling skyward

on an elegant white trellis.

We stood admiring it, summer losing
steam one breezy afternoon,

when a look of amazement bloomed
on her deeply carved face.

Detecting the swell of pride she rushed
to hide, I pretended not to notice this

delicate moment, transient, beyond
her grasp and mine, then offered

my open hand to see her through
a thickening autumn fog.

Missing The Point

My first breath this morning seemed
the same from the night before.

Different at all or just a reference to
the sway of seconds on a tireless clock?

In fact does anything move or do we run in
place believing change is occurring like rain
or snow or wind that pushes through the air,
us, a blanket of anxious eyes convinced we
are on this planet only to do more and more,
seldom pausing, always out of breath?

Not knowing is somehow knowing.

The Art Of Remembering

Stones were scattered about
like oversized tablets bearing
names dates words of passing

as though intending to capture
voices that could be forgotten
in the haste of human survival.

But regardless of size color or
design those weathered stones
failed me, and I couldn't find you

until I stopped looking, sat down
on the ground to recall the color
of your hair and eyes, your hands,

your wistful gaze when life wanted
more from you than you had to give—
then, only then, did I find you.

Hearing A Story

On a cool spring evening
the mourning dove returned.
I'd missed its melancholy refrain:
how I could hear it above
neighborhood lawnmowers,
yelping dogs,
the distant hammering
of shingles on a tattered roof.

Emulating a polite whisper,
the dove's persistent coo
hung in the air
like a coded message
for a concealed dimension,
one just over the rolling hills
north of town,
hills from my childhood imagination
that led me to a landscape
of fine white sand and luminous red lilies
forever suspended, in a stony silence,
by remnants of time.

Rigged Game

Yesterday was easily lost, hardly a strong
sea breeze, the kind that pushed my

old sailboat far from shore. I hauled her
away to slow things down, to keep things

in place but another breeze and another
came along, raking through my churning

thoughts, pushing mountains of moments
into months, years, decades.

Yearning to somehow contain this restless
energy, I stopped doing anything at all

until the air around me grew hot and still,
and suffocating.

Seeing The World

Only a small girl I stood under an apple tree
in my grandmother's yard to watch the clever
sun sliding somewhere, a sense of mystery
rattling in my chest.

Vague and unsettling, the massive yellow orb
was always slipping away, emerging hours later
from the other side of the world. Still round, still
bright, still deeply silent.

Years intervened.

Now the giant fireball carves my days into
morning, noon, and night in one gaping instant,
though I am still rushing to catch the dawn.

Glide

Still a boy he ran along the tracks:
a whistle blew
something was coming
the roar of an engine
the rattle of tracks and steel

running faster, he hoped to beat
the train somehow—his spirit
on fire against a power he
could not name

and with each heavy breath his legs
rowed through time,

feet barely touching the earth.

A Distant Cry

Nothing moves me like the advance of
morning light, ribbons of rose unfurling

into silken threads. Yet I flee south, and
it is quickly high noon, a stringent direction

bleeding into deepening hues of evening,
the imminent gloom of nightfall, and I hold

fast to each long breath. Bones like straw,
I move gingerly with audacious shadows

in a fading light. A final juncture, a quivering
bird released to the other side.

Ancients Of The Earth

Resting under a mangled oak,
thick woody arms stirring steamy air,
a roving bee found me

Waving my hands about,
the buzzing stopped
and I sank deeper into the cool ground
mostly to listen

Yet the world had gone quite still,
what little I knew of it,
what little surrounded me

Shifting my gaze, I stared up into
the tree's private domain of arteries
and veins posing as twitching leaves,
slender brown twigs

With everything rolled into one
dark trunk—rough, smelling of dust
and time itself—I could only wish
to contain it all.

A NOTE FROM THE AUTHOR

I did not grow up loving poetry. I did not even love poetry into early adulthood, so I can't be sure how or why I finally discovered its ability to illuminate the more meaningful layers of life. Now, however, as a poet, my appreciation for this art form only increases. Perhaps it is the incomprehensible abundance of words and opinions in our world that seem to weigh us all down emotionally and spiritually; perhaps we see more of the complexities of existence as we mature. The tangled web of darkness and light, for instance. The human quest for truth in an age of nonsensical proclamations. Whatever it is, poetry seems to reach into the very soul of life in ways often difficult to achieve otherwise. I hope you enjoyed these "poems of time." As a continuation of all that has come before us, we are all "ancients of the earth." —DAH

Write as if you were dying. At the same time, assume you write for an audience consisting solely of terminal patients. That is, after all, the case. What would you begin writing if you knew you would die soon? What could you say to a dying person that would not enrage by its triviality?
— ANNIE DILLARD, THE WRITING LIFE

ABOUT THE AUTHOR

D. A. (Daisy) Hickman published her first nonfiction title in 1999 (William Morrow), but when the world of publishing began to shift significantly, she realized it was becoming important to retain the rights to her creative efforts, so launched her own publishing imprint: Capturing Morning Press. This book of poetry, her first full-length collection, is Hickman's third title under her imprint; she is happily at work on another book of poetry and a new nonfiction title.

Hickman is committed to bringing works of depth and insight forward. Though ample titles are always on the market, there is, simultaneously, a shortage of books that manage to penetrate the "sameness" of our contemporary culture. The author suggests that commercial publishing can suffer from an excessive focus on demanding marketing and financial goals when discerning readers seem to be seeking diverse, thought-provoking perceptions from books that open the heart and mind to something new.

To read a more in-depth interview with the author, please follow this link to Richard Gilbert's blog: http://richardgilbert.me/we-need-memoir/.

Formal Education: M.S., Iowa State University; B.A., Stephens College

Member: Academy of American Poets, South Dakota State Poetry Society

Founder, 2010 @ SunnyRoomStudio.com (a creative sunny space for kindred spirits)

Professional Pursuits: author, poet, publisher, editor, blogger, (previous career emphasis: complex organization, nonprofit management and development)

Published, to date, by Capturing Morning Press:

Ancients of the Earth: Poems of Time (2017)

The Silence of Morning: A Memoir of Time Undone (2015)

Always Returning: The Wisdom of Place (2014)*

Eventually it occurred to me that life is more than an ending. That despite the trauma of my son's loss and everything leading up to it, there IS something more. I will always be a dedicated student of society looking for the essential story, the universal message: a path with less suffering, deeper awareness.

—D.A. Hickman, The Silence of Morning: A Memoir of Time Undone (2015)

Author updates: follow SunnyRoomStudio blog posts, find Daisy on social media, send email to wisdom@sunnyroomstudio.com.

---

* *Where the Heart Resides: Timeless Wisdom of the American Prairie* (William Morrow/Eagle Brook, 1999, first edition)

A NOTE ON THE TYPE

The text of this book was set in Palatino. With its "elegant proportions" and based on the humanist types of the Italian Renaissance, this old-style serif typeface was designed in 1948 by Hermann Zapf (November 8, 1918–June 4, 2015). This classic font is named after the 16th-century Italian master of calligraphy Giambattista Palatino, a contemporary of Leonardo DaVinci. Known for its "strong, open style," Palatino projects a certain "style and grace" often attributed to Zapf's considerable aptitude in calligraphy. Referred to as a "warm, organic design," Zapf's font features the "beauty, harmony, and grace of fine handwriting."

Display text set in Cyan.

www.ingramcontent.com/pod-product-compliance
Lightning Source LLC
Chambersburg PA
CBHW021131300426
44113CB00006B/384